D1534836

The Truth About UFOs
A Scientific Perspective

Written by
Robert M Powell

Cover illustrated by
Reena S Powell

The Truth About UFOs

Printed in the United States of America.

First Edition: 2020

ISBN: 978-1-0878-9149-1

Independently Published

This book is dedicated to Kaleb, Gavin, and Ava, who make me realize that every day God has given us is a blessing.

Contents

Some Interesting UFO Reports (continued)

Preface

This book is written for the young mind that is curious about the world around them and with a desire to learn about everything whether it's insects, games, volcanoes, or airplanes. It is written about a subject that is often misunderstood by adults – UFOs. As your child reads this book, they will learn about more than just UFOs. They will learn how to apply scientific reasoning, new words, and a little science and history in the process. But most importantly, your child will be challenged to think about the world around themselves and not just in black and white, or yes and no. The book shows them that it is important to keep an open mind and that sometimes we must view the world in shades of gray.

In the back of the book is a vocabulary list to help the young reader with any words that might be a challenge.

Did You Know?

UFOs have been seen in every country of the world.

There are over 5000 UFO sightings reported in the United States every year.

More than 1000 military pilots and commercial airline pilots have seen UFOs when they were flying their planes.

Did you know that many famous people have seen UFOs? Presidents Jimmy Carter and Ronald Reagan saw a UFO and even a very famous British prime minister by the name of Winston Churchill.

Nick Jonas of the Jonas Brothers saw a UFO. So did Green Bay quarterback Aaron Rogers. Singer Zayn Malik and his girlfriend Gigi Hadid saw a UFO together.

Sometimes people get scared when they think of UFOs. In 1938 a broadcaster by the name of Orson Welles made up a story that Earth was being invaded by Martians and he broadcast it on the radio as if it was really happening. People believed it was real and they panicked, running into the streets.

UFOs have been reported in every kind of shape that you can imagine: disks, triangles, spheres, cigars, cylinders, boomerangs, pear shapes, rectangles, and even bar bell shapes that you use in the gym!

Some UFOs have been reported as small as a basketball and others have been reported to be larger than a football stadium. That's huge!

People have seen UFOs hover and move without making any noise.

Pilots have reported seeing disk-shaped UFOs flying sideways. How does something fly sideways?!?

Some pilots have seen UFOs that they chased disappear so fast that they were gone in less than a second.

There are thousands of reports about UFOs that would fly into the ocean and fly back out of the ocean. Two of the most common places that happens is near the island of Puerto Rico in the Caribbean

Sea and Catalina Island off the coast of southern California near the city of Los Angeles.

The United States Air Force has tried to shoot down a UFO, which is not a very friendly thing to do. It is good that they failed and it is good that the UFO did not fire back!

Did you know that some people believe that a UFO crashed in Roswell, New Mexico in 1947?

If these facts are interesting to you then keep reading this book and learn more about UFOs. Once you finish reading this book, you will be on your way to becoming a UFO expert!

What is a UFO?

What do you think of when you hear the word UFO? Do you think of aliens or a space ship from another world or do you think of something else? Many people think that UFO is a word that means aliens in a spaceship. But that is not what it means at all. UFO is an abbreviation for the words Unidentified Flying Object. A UFO is an object in the sky that we cannot identify or recognize. So if your friends tell you that

UFO means an alien space ship, you can tell them what it really means.

Have you ever seen an object far away that you could not identify but then when it got closer you could tell what it was? Maybe it was a kite or a plane or a balloon but at first you just thought, "Hmm, I wonder what that is? I'll watch it a little longer and see if I can figure it out." So when you first saw this unknown object flying in the sky, you could truthfully say it was a UFO because you did not know what it was. But once it got closer and you recognized it, it was no longer a UFO. It was an object flying in the sky that you had seen before. This is what we call a IFO, an Identified Flying Object. There are a lot of things in the sky that start off as being a UFO but once you figure out what it is, it becomes a IFO.

Imagine you saw a very bright light moving in the night sky. As it moves across the sky in a controlled path you realize that the light is brighter than any star or planet that you have ever seen before. It's also moving fairly fast but it doesn't have any blinking lights so you know that it's probably not a plane. What could it be? You ask your parents to come outside and look at it. They tell you that maybe it is the International Space Station that orbits the Earth. You do a little research on your own and you find that your parents' guess was right. So what was originally a UFO is now explained. This is a picture of the International Space Station as it looks from space. The reason it is so bright at night is because the sun's light is reflected off all the metal and solar panels that you see in the photo.

International Space Station seen from Space. *(courtesy NASA)*

There are many other examples of objects in the sky that can look strange sometimes. They might seem to be unidentifiable when you first see them but once you know what to look for then you will know they are no longer UFOs.

Before you go to the next page, take some time and write down all of the things you can think of that fly or that shine in the sky and might fool people into thinking they saw a UFO. Try to think of things that could be in the daytime sky and in the nighttime sky. Then turn the page and see how many you found.

Here is a list of five of the most common items that people sometimes don't recognize and think they have seen a UFO:

Satellites; they go around the earth and can sometimes be fairly bright at night,

Stars and Planets; if you stare at a bright star at night for a long time, it will seem like it moves because your eyes play tricks on you – try it yourself sometime,

Airplanes; sometimes at night a plane's blinking lights or a military plane's unusual lights can trick a person into thinking they are seeing something strange,

The Moon; it may be hard to believe but some people have seen the moon behind the clouds and thought it was a UFO,

Birds; when birds are far away and have their wings folded they can look like a flying saucer diving through the sky.

How did you do? Did you write down some of the five most common objects that are not always recognized for what they are, and are thought to be UFOs?

The Truth About UFOs

Sometimes there are objects in the sky that are very very difficult to recognize. What would you think if you saw something bright orange or red in the night sky that looks like what you see in the picture on this page? You might think that was a UFO. Have some fun with this picture. Show it to your parents or friends and ask them if they have seen anything that looks like this. Then ask them if they think these objects are UFOs. Turn the page to find out what the objects are in this picture.

The picture is of two Chinese Lanterns floating through the air at night. Chinese Lanterns are basically plastic bags with a candle in the middle of the bag. It works in the same way as a hot air balloon. When you light the candle then it heats the air and causes the plastic bag to rise in the air.

This is what a Chinese Lantern looks like before it is released into the air.

Never try to create a Chinese Lantern by yourself. They're dangerous and can cause fires when they land.

Sometimes there are objects in the sky that we try everything that we can to explain and they are still a mystery. This is what you call a real UFO – something that remains an unidentified flying object.

The picture on this page is of an object filmed by a plane at Edwards Air Force Base in California. No one has been able to explain what this object could be. It is not a balloon, a Chinese Lantern, an airplane, or any type of missile. Until we can definitely identify this object, it is what we would call a real UFO.

UFO photo. *(courtesy U.S. Air Force)*

Robert Powell

You have learned how a scientist examines an unknown subject. A scientist looks at all the possibilities and eliminates them one by one. If something in the sky cannot be explained in any way, then it can be called a UFO until an explanation is later found. But it cannot be assumed that it is an alien spaceship. We can have ideas and theories that might explain a UFO, but we will talk about that later in the book.

When Did People First See UFOs?

UFOs have been seen throughout history. Over two thousand years ago the Romans reported seeing phantom ships shining in the sky. In the spring of the year 1561 the residents of Nuremberg, Germany described a large black object in the sky that was shaped like a triangle. Were these real UFOs that could not be explained? It is hard to say because there is not much reliable information on what was seen because it happened so long ago.

Beginning in 1942, during the second World War, the first reliable reports of UFOs were first made by American, British, and German pilots in Europe. They described balls of light that would hover off their wing tips and then suddenly fly around their aircraft at incredible speeds. The pilots called these strange lights that followed them, foo fighters. (Did you know there is an American rock band that named themselves after these strange lights? The band is called Foo Fighters.)

These first reports of UFOs began almost eighty years ago – back when your great-grandparents were probably teenagers. No one has a good picture of a foo fighter. The picture below was created based on the descriptions given by the pilots during World War II.

Recreation: World War II Bombers and Foo Fighters

The first famous UFO report that occurred in the United States involved a private pilot by the name of Kenneth Arnold on June 24, 1947. He saw nine thin disk-shaped objects moving through the sky near Mt. Rainier in the state of Washington. He estimated that they were flying at 1800 miles per hour which is four times faster than the planes of 1947 could fly. Soon the newspapers picked up the story and the news was everywhere.

Kenneth Arnold was worried that these disk-shaped objects might be a new aircraft built by an enemy of the United States. The second World War had ended only two years earlier and everyone was worried about whether we could get into a new war with a country called the Soviet Union. The Soviet Union doesn't exist anymore but it was our enemy in 1947. It was made up of a group of countries in Eastern Europe that were controlled by Russia. The Soviet Union and the United States were enemies from the end of World War II until the Soviet Union dissolved into separate countries in 1991. Kenneth Arnold thought that perhaps these objects came from the Soviet Union.

Do you think Kenneth Arnold was right to be worried? The United States Air Force was worried for the same reason. And this was not the only strange aircraft to be seen over U.S. skies. More and more reports came in.

Hundreds of UFOs were seen each year in the 1950s. Back then they didn't call them UFOs, they called them flying saucers. Here is why. The description many people gave was that they looked like two coffee saucers stuck together and flying across the sky.

You can make your own flying saucer at home. Take one coffee saucer and place it on the table but instead of putting a coffee cup on it, put another coffee saucer on it upside down. It should look similar to the picture on this page. Just don't try to glue the saucers together or make it fly. Your parents might not like you to mistreat their coffee saucers. ☺

The year 1952 was especially exciting as people were reporting flying saucers over Washington, D.C., our nation's capital. People were so concerned that stories about flying saucers showed up on the front page of the major newspapers.

Even the president was briefed by the military about the saucers. People became so worried and concerned that an Air Force general went on a special news conference to tell people that everything was okay and that they did not need to worry. His name was General John Samford and he was the Director of Air Force

Intelligence. He said at the news conference, "Credible people have seen incredible things." What did he mean by that? He meant that people that you can depend upon had seen objects in the sky that could make some incredible maneuvers.

It wasn't just the public that was worried about these new objects in the skies. The United States Air Force was also worried about flying saucers so they began investigating reports. They wanted to know if these could be some new aircraft developed by the Soviet Union. So the Air Force created a special group to investigate UFOs, which back then were called flying saucers. They called this new secret organization, Project Blue Book, and its headquarters was at Wright-Patterson Air Force Base in Ohio.

It didn't take the Air Force long to decide that the UFOs were not a new secret weapon developed by the Soviet Union. But they did not know what the UFOs were or where they came from. The Air Force investigated over 12,000 reports and could explain most of them as objects such as a star, an airplane, a bird, etc. But there were more than 700 reports that they could not explain.

UFOs were a complete mystery to the Air Force and they had no reasonable explanation for them. What exactly were these objects? Where did they come from? The Air Force did not know.

The main reason the Air Force first began investigating the UFO phenomenon was they were worried that UFOs might be a threat to our national security. Yet, after investigating UFOs for 22 years, the Air Force had no examples where UFOs had ever intentionally done anything to harm an airplane or a person.

So in 1969 the Air Force closed Project Blue Book and they stopped taking reports from the public about UFOs. But just because the Air Force closed Project Blue Book, this didn't mean the UFOs went away. Reports of UFOs continued, year after year after year. Let's take a look at some of the most interesting cases of the last 70 years.

Robert Powell

Some Interesting UFO Reports

Husband and Wife Photograph a UFO

The sun had already set when Mr. and Mrs. Trent turned into the driveway of their farm in rural Oregon. It was May 11, 1950 and Mrs. Trent had a little folding camera in her lap that she had used to take some family pictures earlier in the afternoon. Cameras were much different in 1950 than they are today. They weren't electronic and you could not instantly see the picture that you had taken. You had to remove a photographic film from the back of the camera, mail it to

a company that would turn your film into a picture, and wait several days before your pictures came back. Here is a picture of what Mrs. Trent's camera looked like. Isn't it strange? Ask your grand parents how one of these

cameras worked and they will probably enjoy telling you some stories.

Mrs. Trent had been feeding her rabbits in the backyard of her home, when she noticed a strange object speeding through the sky. She shouted for her husband who came running from the kitchen with the camera. Mr. Trent dashed outside. Moving in the sky was a bronze, disk-shaped object that he believed was 20 to 30 feet in diameter. It looked like an upside down pie pan with a little antennae on its top. Mr. Trent took two pictures before the object flew away.

The two photos that Mr. Trent took with his camera are shown on the next page. An enlarged picture of the second photo is on the next page after those two photos.

Robert Powell

Do you think that Mr. and Mrs. Trent might have thrown something into the air to make it look like a UFO? All of the people that knew the Trents said that they were very honest people and would not create a hoax. It has been 70 years since the Trents took the photo and still no one knows for sure if that is a real photo of a UFO or not.

Two Air Force Pilots Encounter a Bumble Bee UFO

May 22, 1956. The two Air Force pilots were flying at night. They had left their Air Force base in Greenville, Mississippi and were headed west. They could see the lights of the city of Monroe, Louisiana below them. The men were young lieutenants. Earl Holwadel was 25 years old and was the pilot of the jet. His co-pilot, Curtis Carley, was one year older. They enjoyed flying their jet and this is why they joined the Air Force – to fly jets. They could not be more happy.

The two young men were enjoying the beautiful stars in the night sky when Lieutenant Holwadel noticed a very bright light to their right. It was much too bright to be a star or planet so the young men decided to investigate. They banked their jet to the right towards the light.

Their jet headed straight towards the strange light. Suddenly the light raced towards them but at a speed much faster than the jet. The two pilots were concerned and maybe a little scared. What <u>was</u> this object? The UFO flew right in front of them as it passed by.

T-33 Jet *(Courtesy U.S. Air Force)*

Then it turned around and came flying back towards their jet. The pilots were amazed at how suddenly the UFO could just stop and then come flying back towards them at a high speed. Their jet was not that fast, nor could their jet scamper around the sky as quickly as the UFO.

When the UFO raced towards them the second time, it came very close to them. It shone an intense bright white light at their plane. The light lit up the inside of their jet as if someone had turned on a bright lamp. Imagine what the pilots must have been thinking as this happened.

The two pilots got a very good look at the UFO. It was about 40 feet long and 15 feet high in the middle. There were ribs that extended out from it. Lt. Holwadel drew a picture of what they had seen. He never had been good at drawing. His drawing looked a little like a bumble bee.

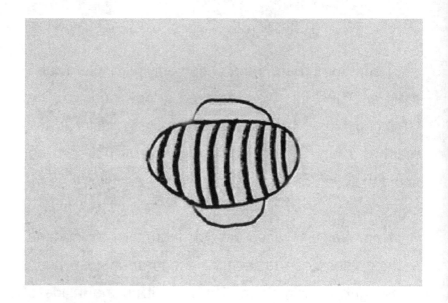

But one thing the two pilots knew for certain, this was not a bumble bee!

A Sheriff and his Deputy Encounter a Large UFO

September 3, 1965. It was about 11 o'clock at night when Sheriff Bob Goode and his Chief Deputy, Billy McCoy, were driving their patrol car southwest of Houston, Texas. Sheriff Goode wasn't feeling very well because earlier in the day a baby alligator had bitten his left finger and it was hurting quite a bit. He didn't realize a baby alligator bite could hurt so much, so he was glad his deputy was with him.

Here is a picture of them taken by the Air Force investigators. Sheriff Goode is on the left and Chief Deputy McCoy is on the right.

The deputy was asking the sheriff how his bite was doing, when he noticed a bright purple light that seemed to be several miles away. The sheriff saw it too and pulled the car to the side of the road so that he and the deputy could look at the purple light through their binoculars. They were carefully looking at the light when suddenly the light began moving towards the officers at a very rapid speed.

In a matter of seconds the object was right in front of them, and only 150 feet away. It was huge. They guessed it was 200 feet wide and 40 feet thick – about the size of a four story warehouse – and just hovering in the air. How could something that big just float in the air? It was dark gray and shaped like a triangle. There was a bright purple light on its left side. Yet this huge object made no noise – it was completely silent.

Then something amazing and disturbing happened. The object in front of them shined a purple light on them. It lit up the inside of their patrol car and all of the surrounding area. Sheriff Goode felt like there was a strong heat coming from the object onto his left arm.

After a few seconds the sheriff and deputy became scared and they got back in their car and drove off. They drove as fast as they could go, sometimes at speeds up to 110 miles per hour! Deputy McCoy kept watching the object and was glad to see that it wasn't following them.

Here is a drawing that the deputy made of the object that he and the sheriff saw.

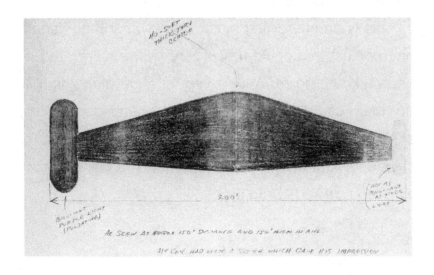

The sheriff and deputy went back to their job of patrolling until about 4 o'clock in the morning when they decided to stop at a cafe for breakfast. As they ate their breakfast, Sheriff Goode noticed that his alligator bite on his left finger was no longer sore. He was happy about that but was somewhat surprised so he unwrapped the bandage to look at it. He discovered that the swelling had gone down and the wound was nearly healed. The next day, the wound showed almost no scars. This was the same hand that had gotten warm when the UFO shined the purple light on it.

This is an interesting story. The lawmen had seen a huge object that could travel very fast, hover in the air and make no noise. And, a very strange purple light lit up their car. What do you think happened to the sheriff's alligator bite? Did it heal up because the UFO shined its light on his arm or was it just a coincidence? Why would the UFO do that?

A Young Boy Sees a Mushroom-Shaped UFO

November 2, 1971. It was a pleasant autumn evening as sixteen year old Ronald Johnson checked on the sheep at his family's farm. The sun had set just over an hour ago and the stars were now all out. It was a beautiful starry night. At least it was until Ron heard this loud noise that sounded like an old washing machine rattling. He looked towards the sound and saw a glowing object emitting many different colors. It was hovering about two feet above the ground and was only 75 feet away. Ron said it was so close that he could have hit it with a rock.

The noisy object looked a little like a large mushroom except that it was ten feet tall, almost twice as tall as Ron. The object had a dome on the top and was more narrow at the bottom. The entire mushroom-looking "thing" glowed but there was an extra bright light that came from its bottom that lit up the ground beneath it. Ron said that the light was so bright that it hurt his eyes to look at it.

After a few minutes the bottom of the object got very bright and the object rose up and moved above the farm shed. The rattling noise it made changed to a high pitch whine just before it took off into the night sky. Ron called for his parents to come out and look but by the time they came out, all that was left to see was a bright light in the sky.

Here is a drawing made of the strange UFO.

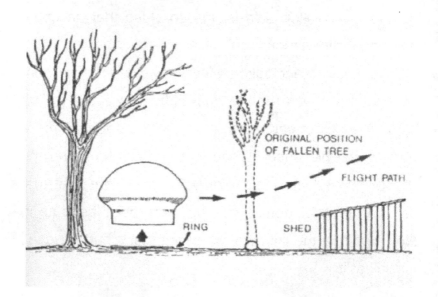

After the light in the sky disappeared, Ron turned to show his parents where the object had hovered just above the ground. They all saw something startling. Where the object had hovered was now a large glowing white ring on the ground. The soil itself was glowing! Ron's mother noticed a white crystal-like powder on the soil and touched it. The powder caused her finger to burn slightly and to go numb where she touched it. Ron's parents wanted a picture of this ring. They went back into their house, retrieved their camera, and took a picture of the glowing soil.

The next day, Ron and his parents reported what happened to the Sheriff's office. Mrs. Johnson showed the picture of the soil ring that glowed in the dark to the sheriff. So the sheriff went with the Johnsons back to their farm so that he could see for himself. Sure enough, there was a very distinct ring at their farm about eight feet across. He took a sample and found the soil to be almost white and very dry as compared to the surrounding soil. There was no plant life or animal life in the area of the ring. It was very strange.

The soil samples were tested by many different universities and government agencies. No one could determine exactly what had happened to the soil to make it glow. Perhaps the theory from Texas A&M University might provide the best answer. They guessed that the soil change and its dry condition could have been caused by exposure to very high microwave energy. The same type of energy that is produced in your microwave oven, except 20,000 times as powerful. Could the mushroom-shaped UFO have been emitting microwaves into the soil as it hovered? No one knows. Maybe someday someone will find out.

Four Army Reserve Soldiers Meet a UFO up Close in their Helicopter

October 18, 1973. This is one of the strangest UFO stories that you will hear and it involved four very reliable military witnesses.

A four-man crew in an Army Reserve Huey helicopter took off at about 10:30 pm from Cleveland, Ohio. It was a clear, calm, and starry night as they flew over woody rolling hills and farmland. Lieutenant Jezzi was flying the helicopter and Captain Coyne was sitting next to him in the co-pilot seat. Sitting in the back seats were Sergeants Yanacsek and Healey.

Bell UH-1 (courtesy U.S. Army)

After flying for about 30 minutes, Sergeant Yanacsek noticed a bright red light that seemed to be following the helicopter at a distance. Soon all the soldiers saw the light. Suddenly the light began to fly directly towards their helicopter at a high rate of speed. Captain Coyne was worried the light might be from a plane on a collision course with the helicopter so he took over the controls and began to dive downwards towards the ground to avoid a collision with the plane. The light continued towards them even as they dove downwards. They were about to collide head-on! The men braced for a crash.

Suddenly the other aircraft stopped just in front and above the helicopter. The men could tell it was not an airplane. A gray cigar-shaped object was in front of them. It was so close to their helicopter that all they could see through their front windshield was the object. All four soldiers stared in awe as their minds tried to understand what was happening and what they were seeing. There was a red light at the nose of the cigar-shaped object, a white light at its rear, and a strange green light beam that was being emitted from the lower part of the object.

The green beam of light swung downwards towards the soldiers. It lit up the entire interior of their helicopter.

Everything inside appeared green from the intense light. And Captain Coyne noticed something odd – his compass was spinning like crazy.

Just as suddenly as the cigar-shaped object had moved towards them, it began to move away. Within seconds it was nothing but a bright white light far away. But something strange had happened during all the excitement. Captain Coyne noticed that while the object was next to them it had pulled his helicopter higher and away from the ground. His helicopter was now twice as high in the air as it had been before. The captain had no explanation for how this could have happened because the helicopter controls were still in the downward position. Either the pilot had made some serious error or the cigar-shaped UFO had pulled their helicopter upwards.

This story raises a lot of questions because of the strange things that happened. How does an object fly towards them at a high speed and suddenly stop in front of them? Why did the compass spin like crazy? A compass points toward a magnetic field. Could the

UFO have been emitting a magnetic field? And did the helicopter really get pulled higher into the air? If it did, why would the UFO have caused that? There are so many questions that are unanswered about what happened to these four soldiers.

What is in common with this story and some of the earlier stories? Do you remember how the pilots over Louisiana had a bright white light shine on their jet and how the sheriff and deputy had a bright purple light shine into their car? What other things are common in these stories? As you continue to read, think back about how some parts of these stories are similar.

Two F-4 Phantom Jets Race Towards a UFO

September 18, 1976. This story takes place in Iran near its capital city, Tehran. You have probably heard about the country of Iran on TV as an enemy of America, but in the year 1976 they were our friends. The Iranians flew the most reliable American-made jets that we had – the F-4 Phantom. The Phantom is a beautiful jet as you can see in the photo. Although they were first built in the 1960s, they could fly almost as fast as most modern military jets. The F-4 Phantom could fly twice as fast as the speed of sound. That is over 1500 miles per hour.

F-4 Phantoms *(courtesy U.S. Air Force)*

It was late at night when a UFO showed up above the city of Tehran. People were calling the airport and pilots of passenger planes also reported the strange object. The control tower at the airport called the Iranian Air Force and reported the unknown object that was in the skies above them. The general on duty called a nearby air base and requested that jets be sent to investigate.

Lieutenant Parviz Jafari's F-4 Phantom jet rocketed down the runway at 1:30 in the morning. He was a young man, only 23 years old and his heart was beating fast as he pushed his jet to its maximum speed of twice the speed of sound. At that speed he could travel 24 miles in only one minute. It would take him only three minutes to reach the UFO. But as he sped towards the object it began to speed away from him. It was much faster than his jet. He couldn't catch it so his commander ordered him back to the base.

Lieutenant Parvis Jafari by his jet

Lt. Jafari turned his plane around and began his short trip back to the airfield in Tehran. But once he turned around, the UFO also turned around and began to chase his plane. The pilot reported to the base in a distressed voice, "Something is coming at me from behind. It is 15 miles away...now ten miles...now five miles. It is level now...I think it is going to crash into me. It has just passed me by...missing me narrowly." The UFO had passed the jet and was again hovering north of the city of Tehran.

Lt. Jafari again approached the UFO with his jet. He was within 29 miles of the UFO and in one more minute his jet would reach it. Suddenly his radio and all his instrument panels went out. Without his navigation control and running low on fuel, he was forced to turn around and return to his air base. Oddly, as soon as he turned around he regained his radio and instrument panel controls. He returned to the air base and landed his plane.

But the Iranians were not done. They launched another jet to intercept the UFO. The pilot detected the object on his radar which showed the UFO to be three to four times as large as his jet. As the pilot got closer to the object it began to jump around in the sky so quickly that he could not keep up with it. But the jet didn't give up chasing the UFO until something unexpected again happened.

A smaller and very bright object came out of the UFO and headed straight for the jet. The pilot reacted. He thought that perhaps some type of weapon had been launched at him. The pilot decided to fire a missile at the approaching object. Before he could fire his missile all of his instrument panels went out, just like what happened to the first jet. Unable to fire his missile, the pilot tried to get away from the object headed towards him. He made a sharp turned and headed back to his base. Once he did that the object followed him for a while and then it returned to the larger UFO and rejoined with it. The UFO remained in the area a while longer before disappearing from sight.

Both jets lost control of their instrument panels. Did the UFOs cause it or was it a coincidence? Do you think the UFOs acted friendly or unfriendly? Did the Iranian F-4 jets act friendly or unfriendly? What would you have done differently?

Policemen in Memphis See a Triangle-Shaped UFO

May 17, 1977. A total of six police officers saw a triangle-shaped UFO in Memphis, Tennessee on a warm spring night. It all began when policeman Davidson was talking to his two fellow officers and looked up into the sky to see a strange object. The policeman said, "Look there's a flying saucer!" At first the other two officers thought he was joking until Davidson said, "Look! I'm not kidding!" What the three officers saw looked nothing like a flying saucer. This object was shaped like a triangle and made no noise as it moved through the sky. One of the policemen said it was "Lit up like a Christmas tree." It had white, yellow, and bright orange lights. The policemen watched it for about a minute before it flew out of sight.

One hour later the triangle-shaped object was seen by a highway patrol officer near Collierville, a small town just outside of Memphis and towards the southeast. But the most exciting encounter between this object and the police was still to come.

Several hours later at 3:30 in the morning, officers Jerry Jeter and Troy Todd were driving on the freeway in an unmarked police van in Memphis. It was a normal night until officer Todd noticed some red and green lights on an object hovering just above two high voltage towers. At first they thought it might be a helicopter and were worried why a helicopter would be flying so close to the electrical lines. So they turned their van around on the freeway and went back to investigate.

Officer Jerry Jeter

Officer Troy Todd

When the policemen got back to where they had first seen the lights, there was nothing there. But soon they spotted the lights on the other side of the freeway. They pulled their van off the highway and got out to look at the object more closely. It was shaped like a triangle and it was huge. It was as long as a football field and as thick as two houses stacked on top of each other. It had white, red, and green lights on it and it had a white glow around it. This huge UFO just sat still in the air and it made no sound. What happened next will surprise you.

The officers took their rifle out of the van. But they weren't going to shoot at the UFO. They wanted to use the scope on their rifle so that they could look more closely at it. As they watched it through the scope, the UFO began to slowly move away. As it began to move, all of the lights went out except for the white glow around the object. Then two red lights came on in the back of the UFO. Suddenly the UFO sped away at a tremendous rate of speed and amazingly disappeared over the horizon in just one to two seconds.

It was time for the policemen to report what they had seen to headquarters. Todd didn't want to call dispatch because as he told Jeter, "They'll think we're crazy."

Jeter's response was, "What the heck, let's call. I don't give a s***." So Jeter called dispatch at their downtown headquarters and reported what had happened.

This is an amazing story. Should we believe it? Would all of these policemen make up a story? A newspaper reporter investigated the incident. He talked to their supervisor, police Lieutenant Jim Pugh, and asked about the five policemen. Lieutenant Pugh replied, "Yes sir. They have worked for me for five years and they are all good police officers. If they said they saw it, I believe they saw it. I would not doubt their word."

Japanese Airlines Flight Sees UFO Over Alaska

November 17, 1986. You don't expect to see a UFO when flying across the ocean in a jet but that is exactly what happened to Captain Kenju Terauchi and his co-pilot. They were about to see something that they would never forget.

The Japanese Airline jet was flying from Paris, the capital of France, to Tokyo, the capital of Japan. As the jet flew over Alaska, the pilots noticed some strange lights that flew alongside them. They called the radio tower to see if there were any other planes near them. The answer came back, "No."

The lights continued to follow the jet for seven to eight minutes but then something strange happened. Captain Terauchi said the lights began to move around in the sky like two bear cubs playing with each other. Then suddenly they weren't just lights anymore. Two square-shaped objects suddenly were directly in front of the jet. They were so bright that their light brightened the inside of the jet and the captain felt heat from the light. The pilots were in awe of what they were seeing. This object was huge.

Captain Terauchi made a drawing of one of the objects that they saw and he also drew the size of his jet to the right of the object.

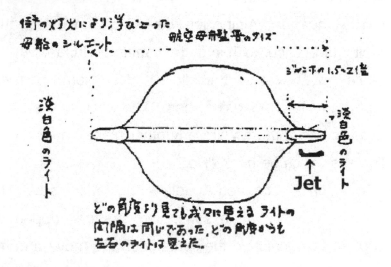

With the object hanging motionless in the air directly in front of them, the pilots tried to contact the control tower. But with the two objects very close to the jet, the radio wouldn't work. Then as suddenly as the two objects appeared, they disappeared and again became lights that were following the jet. Once the objects left, the radio began to work again and the captain called the radio tower.

The operator at the radio tower could see the object on radar and asked the pilot if he wanted military jets scrambled to find the objects. The captain said, "No." He didn't think that was a good idea. After all, what could a military jet do against an object so large and that could move so fast.

The strange objects continued to follow the Japanese jet until it landed in Anchorage, Alaska. The two pilots were very happy to be back on the ground. This was not the type of flight that they had wanted or had expected.

Some people think that the pilots saw a planet in the sky. Do you think that would explain what happened? Would you have asked for military jets to be scrambled if you had been the pilot? Why or why not? Why do you think the UFOs were following the jet? Tell your parents this story and get their opinion.

Triangle-Shaped UFOs Chased by Police and F-16s in Belgium

Beginning in November of 1989 and continuing for almost a year, UFOs shaped like triangles were seen in the country of Belgium, a small country to the north and west of France and Germany. The reports came from everywhere. Firemen, university professors, military soldiers, 13 policemen, and many other people reported seeing strange triangle-shaped craft in the sky. During the evening and night of November 29, almost 250 people saw UFOs at different locations. It would take too long to tell you what all of these 250 people saw but some of the more interesting reports are worth telling.

The sun had just set and the sky was beginning to darken. Two policemen were on patrol when they noticed a field that was lit up. There was a bright light shining on the field. The light was coming from the sky. The police were curious. What was this light and who was shining it? The policemen pulled their car over to the side of the road so that they could investigate.

They got out of their car and looked up. Above them were three very bright white lights on each corner of a huge triangle-shaped object. It was just floating in the air. In the middle of the triangle was a bright pulsating orange light. Here is a picture of a model of the object created by a different witness who had seen a similar object.

The police called their police station to report what they were seeing. At first the policeman answering the phone at the police station thought they were joking but the other policeman said, "No, we're serious."

Meanwhile, the object began to slowly move away. The policemen told their police station that they were going to follow the object. It was easy for them to follow the object in their car because the triangle-shaped UFO was moving so slowly.

Back at the police station the policeman answering the phone looked out his window. He was wondering if there was anything out there or if those other policemen were just crazy. As he peered out the window, he could see a bright light but it was too far away to tell what it was.

Suddenly he saw what looked like a laser beam shoot out of the light and then come back into the light. He realized that the policemen who he had just talked to were not crazy. He had no idea what he was seeing but the policemen following the object got to see the laser light show up close.

The triangle-shaped object that was followed by the police car came to a stop over another field. The policemen stopped their car and got out. They were about to be surprised.

On each side of the object, a red laser beam was shining towards the ground. Between the lasers was a ball of red light that moved towards the ground and then would move back into the object. It would repeat this movement several times. One of the policemen thought that the red ball of light was like some type of camera system that was looking for something.

The policemen continued to watch the object for several minutes when they were surprised to see a second object rise up into the sky. It looked exactly like the other object. The second object tilted over slightly and they could see that there was a small dome on its top. There were also what looked like windows with lights on the inside. Before they could get a better look, both objects moved away and were soon gone.

Stop for a moment and think about what you've read. Does this triangle-shaped object seem similar to what the policemen in Memphis saw 12 years earlier? How was it the same and how was it different? Remember how this huge object just floated silently in the air. Do we have any huge objects that can float silently in the air? Think about whether this could explain what all these people saw. Would you have followed the UFO in your car like the two Belgium policemen did?

Four months after this event, on March 30, 1990, the triangle-shaped UFOs came back again. This time it was the Belgium Air Force that chased them.

Several people at a home saw some unusual triangle-shaped lights moving around in the night sky. They called the police station. The police then called the Belgium Air Force who confirmed that the sightings were real because four different Belgium radar stations detected the objects on radar. With all of this information, the Belgian Air Force scrambled two F-16 jets.

The F-16s took off from the runway. Their mission was to locate and identify the objects picked up on radar at the Air Force bases. The F-16s also have their own radar on the jet. They found the UFOs on their radar screen and chased after them. As the jets got close to the UFOs, the UFOs flew off at speeds too fast for the jets to catch them. The jets tried again. They found the UFOs on their radar again. They started to get close. This time they might catch them. But no, the UFOs flew off again at speeds much too fast for the F-16s. This went on for almost an hour as if the UFOs wanted to play a game of cat and mouse or hide and seek. Finally the UFOs seemed to get tired of the game and left.

A picture of the UFO on the jet's radar screen is shown on the next page. You are looking at the same image that the pilot saw. Imagine that you are the pilot. In the very middle of the radar image you can see a little diamond shaped dot. That is the image of the UFO. Below the diamond you see a number that says 990K. That meant the UFO was traveling at 990 knots (more than 1000 miles per hour) which is much faster than the speed of sound, or about twice as fast as a passenger jet. What was really amazing is that it took the UFO only five seconds to go from 0 to 990 knots. This is at least six times faster than the length of time that it takes an F-16 jet to reach a speed of 990 knots.

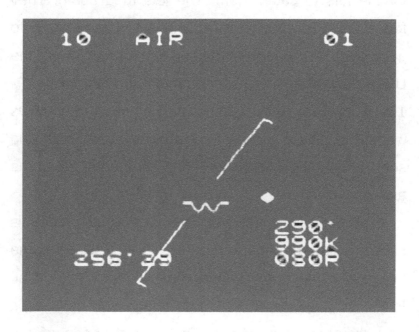

U.S. Navy Jets Intercept a UFO

Probably the most interesting UFO case of modern times happened during November of 2004. It involved the U.S. Navy and its most powerful ships and aircraft. Before you hear the story, you should learn a little about what is called a U.S. Navy Carrier Strike Force.

A Navy Strike Force centers around an aircraft carrier. An aircraft carrier is like a small city in the ocean. It has more than 6,000 people on board. It is the length of more than three football fields. It is so large that jets can land and take off from the aircraft carrier. It can hold 75 aircraft including jets, helicopters, and larger planes. It can travel anywhere in the world. If you want to see an aircraft carrier someday, they can be found in places such as San Francisco, San Diego, New York City, Charleston, and Norfolk, Virginia. Ask your parents to show you one.

There are also other ships that travel with the aircraft carrier: a guided missile cruiser, an attack submarine, two destroyers, supply ships and many jets. This group of planes and ships can detect anything in the ocean and the sky for more than 300 miles. A Navy Strike Group is probably the most powerful military attack group in the world. Below is a photo of a Navy Strike Group. Amazing, isn't it?

U.S. Navy Carrier Strike Group (courtesy U.S. Navy)

So what do you think happened when a Navy Strike Force encountered a UFO? It is an interesting story.

Commander David Fravor and his Lieutenant Commander, James Slaight, were Navy pilots. Both of them had gone to college at the U.S. Naval Academy. It is very difficult to get into the U.S. Naval Academy. You must have very good grades, be in very good physical condition, and you must love to compete. Once they graduated, they learned to fly the most advanced F-18, what the Navy calls the "Super-Hornet". The pilots also learned how to take off and land their jet on an aircraft carrier in the middle of the ocean.

It was November of 2004 and their jet squadron, known as the Black Aces, were assigned to an aircraft carrier named the USS *Nimitz*. Near the aircraft carrier was another ship, a missile cruiser called the USS *Princeton*. One of their jobs was to use their radar system to know about everything in the sky around the Navy Strike Group.

For several days the Senior Chief over radar on the USS *Princeton* had been noticing some very strange objects showing up on his radar screen. They were traveling at an extremely high altitude of more than 80,000 feet . The Senior Chief wondered what these objects might be because one of his jobs was to ensure the safety of the Navy jets. He wasn't too worried because the jets from the USS *Nimitz* didn't fly that high so there was no danger that there might accidentally be a mid-air crash of some sort.

Things changed on November 14. The Senior Chief saw the objects on his radar as usual. But this day was different. He was watching his radar as the objects dropped from over 80,000 feet to only 20,000 feet in less than a second. This worried him. The Senior Chief asked the Captain of the ship if they could request some of the jets from the *Nimitz* check out what was showing up on radar. The Captain said, "Yes."

Commander Fravor and Lieutenant Commander Slaight were already flying in their jets when they received the request to check out what was seen on the USS *Princeton's* radar. They turned their two jets towards the unknown radar target. They didn't know what to expect. Was this going to be an enemy jet? Could it be a passenger jet that was in trouble? They didn't know.

F-18, VFA-41 Black Aces *(courtesy of U.S. Navy)*

This is an image of an F-18 from Commander Fravor's squadron, the VFA-41 Black Aces. It is one of the most successful jets that the Navy has ever flown. The F-18 is still flown by the Navy today. When the two jets got to their destination, they began to fly around looking for something. What they were looking for – they didn't know. At almost the same time both pilots saw a strange disturbance in the water below. At first they were worried that maybe a plane had crashed and was sinking in the water. As they stared at the water disturbance, they noticed another object. It was just above the water and it also seemed to be interested in whatever was beneath the water.

It was flying around but it didn't have any wings, or engines, or helicopter blades, or anything that would be used to fly. It looked like one of those little white candy tic-tacs. But it was much bigger. It appeared to be the same size as their jets, but it was much quicker than a jet. It could change directions like a ping pong ball bouncing around. It was unbelievable. A drawing of what they saw is shown below.

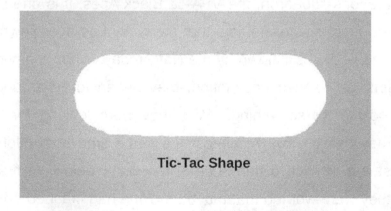

Tic-Tac Shape

Commander Fravor decided to investigate. He didn't have any weapons on his plane but that did not stop him. He was too curious and his gut feeling was that the tic-tac was not a threat. He had Lieutenant Commander Slaight stay at a higher altitude and watch while he flew his jet downwards to the ocean where the tic-tac shaped object was flying. As he flew lower and lower, Fravor saw a change in movement of the tic-tac shaped UFO that told him it knew he was coming. Suddenly, the tic-tac stopped darting around. It turned its nose towards the jet. As the jet began dropping down towards the tic-tac, it began flying upwards towards the jet. The Commander's heart was pounding. He wasn't scared – he was excited. He wanted to know more about this strange object.

As the jet and the UFO kept getting closer and closer, Commander Fravor decided to dive his jet towards the tic-tac shaped object. He plunged his jet downwards to intercept the tic-tac. He was only seconds away from the UFO. Suddenly, the tic-tac moved its nose-end to a different direction. Before the Commander could realize what was happening, the tic-tac flew off at an unbelievable speed. It traveled so fast that it was gone in just one to two seconds. The

Commander was amazed and speechless. How could anything disappear so fast?! Because he was a jet fighter pilot and loved flying fast aircraft, he had a strange thought. He wished he could fly one of those things some day. What an experience that would be!

The UFO was gone. So the two jets flew back to the aircraft carrier. After they landed, the Commander went in search of the next F-18 pilots in his squadron that would be flying. He told the pilots of the next two jets ready for take-off to try and get a video of the tic-tac shaped UFO if they could find it. They said they would try and find it. The two jets screeched down the aircraft carrier runway and headed toward the location where the tic-tac was last seen.

When those two jets returned to the aircraft carrier, one of them had a video of the tic-tac shaped object. On the next page is a still image taken from the video. The tic-tac is the object on the left side of the screen with an arrow pointing at it. This picture is just before the tic-tac zipped away, which can be seen in the video.

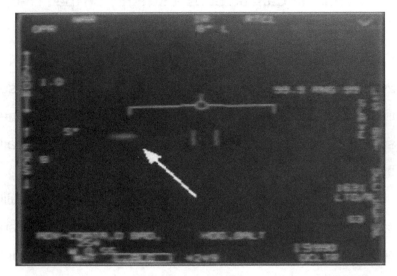

Infra-red Image of the Tic-Tac *(courtesy of U.S. Navy)*

If you want to see the full video, then google or go to YouTube and search for the words "SCU", "Nimitz", "UFO", and "video." You can also go to this site to see the full video:

https://www.explorescu.org/post/nimitz_strike_group_2004

Imagine if you had been Commander Fravor. Would you have flown your jet down towards that tic-tac shaped UFO? Was his decision the right or wrong decision? Talk to your parents and get their thoughts.

Scientist in Canada Sees a Strange Shaped UFO

This will be the last example of our interesting UFO cases. This incident happened just a few years ago in 2013 in Ontario, Canada. The main witness in this case is a scientist who has many different inventions. The scientist doesn't want his real name used so we will call the scientist Gavin.

It was late August. Gavin and his two friends, we will call them Kaleb and Wade, were hunting black bears on some land that Kaleb owned. They were in the middle of a forest and were far far away from any town. They didn't even have a cell phone signal they were so distant from everything. A true wilderness. There is a picture on the next page of what the area looked like during the daytime.

The three men got into their truck. It was getting late. It was 9:40 pm and the skies were very dark with the stars shining. They had to be careful because there were no lights anywhere and the road was just made of dirt. Kaleb was driving, Wade was in the front passenger seat, and Gavin was sitting in the back.

The truck slowly went around a bend in the road and up a hill. It was the exact road and bend in the road that you see in the picture. Kaleb was concentrating on the road ahead. He didn't notice what the scientist in the back seat saw. Off to the right, Gavin could see some unusual lights flying low over the trees. He thought that it could be a helicopter. But why would a helicopter be flying in the middle of nowhere in the middle of the night?

The lights began to come directly towards the truck. Gavin's window was rolled down but he could not hear a thing. He should have been able to hear a helicopter.

His scientific curiosity was peeked. Why was there no noise?

Gavin said to Kaleb, "Stop the truck." Gavin took out his Sony camera so that he could video what was happening. He turned the camera on but as soon as it came on, it would immediately power off. He tried this over and over with the same result. He wanted a video of this object because it had come close enough to the men that they knew it was not a helicopter or anything else that they had ever seen.

Kaleb exclaimed, "Look, it has a huge tail of sparkles or fire." And it did. The sparkles were coming out of the rear of the craft. But this was no ordinary looking aircraft. It had a fat disk on each end with a bar connecting them. It looked like a flying barbell! Lights were revolving around each disk and there was a purple glow that was all around the craft.

This thing was huge. It was 170 feet long and as tall as a house. Its surface looked like shiny metal and there were these very dark black bands around the disks. It was moving slowly over the tree tops and it was so close that they could have hit it with a rock. But the crazy thing was that it made no sound.

Gavin grabbed his phone to take a picture but it had turned itself off just like the Sony camera. He tried the Sony again. It turned on and then turned off, just like before.

Desperate to get a closer look at this amazing flying machine, Gavin took out his rifle which had a 9x scope on it. He excitedly said to Kaleb and Wade, "There is no way that thing can shut off my rifle scope!"

Wade was very excited and asked Gavin if he could shoot the craft. Gavin said, "I'm not going to shoot something when I don't know what it is." But Wade yelled back, "Shoot it. Just shoot it!" Gavin knew that would be a stupid thing to do. He was not going to shoot at it.

Gavin spent the next minute or two closely observing the craft through his rifle scope. He wanted to see if there was any indication that this might be some new kind of military aircraft. He looked for screws and bolts that would tell him it was made by people but none were found. The surface was as smooth as glass. It was so smooth that he could see the stars of the night sky reflecting off the metal.

Gavin continued to watch the craft as it slowly moved away from them. He noticed that although it was traveling in a straight line, it was making a constant zigzag movement as it traveled. The sparkles continued to be emitted from the back of the craft as it zigzagged along, moving farther and father away.

Gavin let Kaleb and Wade look through his rifle scope. While Kaleb looked through the scope and described what he was seeing, Gavin grabbed his Sony camera again and turned it on. This time it stayed on! He pushed the record button. The camera was running but the screen was showing "black". Gavin grabbed his cell phone again to power it up but it was hot and the battery was drained of power. Gavin asked Kaleb to call another truck in the area using his Motorola radio (this is like a high power walkie-talkie). Kaleb answered, "The radio is dead."

The barbell-shaped object continued to move farther away until it disappeared from sight. There was nothing left to do but continue back down the dirt road towards the main highway to their cabin.

When the men got to their cabin that night, Gavin did what any scientist would do. He wrote down notes of what he had seen with his eyes through his rifle scope while it was still fresh in his memory.

They all talked about what had happened. Their Motorola radio was dead due to some type of electrical failure. The cell phone worked again once it was charged up. The Sony camera had recorded their voices but the video screen was just scrambled. They tested the Sony camera and it was working again at the cabin. The men tried to make sense of what they had experienced.

The next week Gavin had one of the engineers that worked for him create a detailed drawing of what he had seen. On the next page is a reproduction of the object that was seen that night.

What do you think of the shape of the object? How can something shaped like that fly? It is strange that there were so many problems with the phone, radio, and camera. Could the strange barbell-shaped craft have been emitting some type of energy that interfered with the equipment? And how about how the men reacted. If you had been Gavin, would you have tried to shoot at the object?

Where Do UFOs Come From?

Do you remember in the beginning of the book that we discussed how a person should not assume that a UFO is an alien spaceship? We cannot say that a UFO is an alien spaceship unless we can prove it. We can think there is a possibility that UFOs are alien spaceships and we can put together ideas as to why we think that is true and we can develop plans and experiments on how we can prove it.

Scientists call a proposed explanation for something that is observed, a hypothesis. Here is an example of a hypothesis: "Earthworms like to live in the shade." You can test your hypothesis by creating a box filled with dirt and cover half the box in shade and leave the other half in the sunlight. If your hypothesis is true then at the end of each day, you will find more earthworms on the shady side of the box. If your hypothesis is not true then you will either find more earthworms on the sunny side of the box or you will find that they are everywhere and it makes no difference. This is one way to test a hypothesis.

There are several different hypotheses that people have proposed to explain UFOs. Some people think that they are all in people's imagination. Other people think that UFOs are created by people from the future. Others think that they might be from a different dimension. But the hypothesis that we will examine is none of those. We will examine the hypothesis that UFOs are controlled by an intelligence from another world. This doesn't mean there are aliens in the UFOs. Maybe there are or maybe they are drones, like a radio controlled airplane that you fly. So let's look at the hypothesis that "UFOs are controlled by an intelligence from another world."

Could UFOs come from a world in our solar system? The closest worlds to Earth are Mars, Venus, and Mercury. Plus, there are the larger planets that are farther away. We have sent space craft to all of these worlds and so far we have not found any life. They are all too cold, too hot, or they don't have air to breathe.

We cannot say it is impossible but we can say that it is very very unlikely that UFOs come from somewhere in our solar system.

Could UFOs come from worlds that orbit others stars? At the time when your parents were born, we didn't know of any other planets that existed other than those in our solar system. Today, we know of more than 4,000 planets that orbit other stars. We call them exo-

Hubble photo of a galaxy with billions of stars and planets (courtesy of ESA and NASA)

planets. We are finding hundreds of new exoplanets every year. It is estimated that there are 11 billion earth-sized planets in our galaxy that orbit stars like our sun. So there are many many planets where life could develop.

Could there be intelligent life on some of these planets? Many scientists think so. This is why we have a program called SETI (Search for Extra-Terrestrial Intelligence). Scientists try to listen if there are any radio messages coming to us from a planet around one of these stars. We know that water is very important for life and we know that water exists on other planets. Many scientists think that given time, life will begin on a planet that has water, the right temperature, and air to breathe. And given more time, that life will evolve into an intelligent species. Do we know for certain that life will evolve on other planets? No. But it is a reasonable hypothesis based on what we know.

If some of those 11 billion planets have an intelligent civilization like ours, would they be able to travel to Earth? This is the big question. So that you will have an idea of how far away the stars are, we will see how long it takes to travel to the nearest star.

Did you know that the closest star to the earth is a sun called Proxima Centauri? Here is a photograph of the star taken by the Hubble space telescope.

The Star Proxima Centauri *(courtesy of ESA and NASA)*

Two planets have already been found that orbit Proxima Centauri. You can't see the planets in the photo because they are too small and too far away. One of those planets is the same size as Earth. It is the right distance from its star to have the right temperature for water to exist. We don't yet know if there is any life on either of those planets.

The Proxima Centauri solar system is about 4 "light years" distant from Earth. So how far away is a "light year"? First, to answer that question, we need to learn a little bit about light.

Have you turned on a flashlight and noticed how fast the light moves across the room? It is so fast you cannot see it move. But it actually does move. Light moves so fast that it will travel 186,282 miles in one second. If you were to shine a powerful light at the moon, it would take less than two seconds for it to reach the moon. That is about the same amount of time that it takes you to inhale a deep breath of air. That's fast because it takes our spaceships three days to get to the moon. That same beam of light would take three minutes to reach the planet Mars and just over an hour to reach the ringed planet Saturn.

Imagine how far that beam of light would travel in one year. Well that distance is what we call a "light year" – the distance a beam of light will travel in one year. So if you took your powerful light and aimed it at the star Proxima Centauri, it would take four years before it reached that sun and its planets. If we tried to send our fastest spaceship to Proxima Centauri, it would take 17,000 years to get there.

But imagine if we could send a spaceship to Proxima Centauri at the speed of light. It would only take four years to get there. Is it possible for a spaceship to travel that fast? We don't know yet, but we actually have plans to some day send a very very tiny spaceship at one-fifth the speed of light to Proxima Centauri and take pictures of its planets. It will take it 20 years to get there.

But remember, Proxima Centauri is the closest star to us. Many of the stars are hundreds of "light years" away from us. So it would take a beam of light hundreds of years to reach those stars.

So back to the big question – could another intelligent civilization send a spaceship to Earth? It appears to be possible and if they are much more advanced than us, they may know other ways to send a spacecraft through space at even faster speeds.

So a hypothesis that UFOs may originate from a planet on another star seems reasonable. That doesn't mean the hypothesis is true, only that it is logical to consider it.

The next step is to begin to collect data to prove the hypothesis. This means we would need to use radar and other methods to first try and determine if UFOs travel from Earth back into space and if they do, which star are they traveling towards. Once we collect that type of data then we will have completed the first step in determining if our hypothesis that UFOs come from other worlds in our universe might be true.

How Can I Learn More About UFOs

I hope that you have enjoyed this book and I hope that it has increased your interest in the subject of UFOs. If it has, you may want to read more books and learn more about the subject. There are several things that you can do to become more knowledgeable.

First, learn more about science. After all, the study of UFOs is like the study of many topics. You need science knowledge to be able to properly analyze a subject. So learn more about science in school. Study the science of the earth, which is called geology. Study the science of the elements, which is called chemistry. Study the science of living things, which is called biology. Study the science of matter and energy, which is learned in physics. Study the science of the stars, which is learned in astronomy. And study how things work, which is found in engineering. You may not be able to learn all of these things, but study the ones that interest you the most.

Second, read more books about UFOs, but be careful what you read. Many books on UFOs have not been well researched and the information in them is not verified. Try to find books that are written by scientists or historians that have done a thorough job of investigating the subject. Here is a list of books that are well written and that you might enjoy reading. They are listed from the easiest to read to the most difficult. So try to read the ones at the beginning of the list first. They should all be available on Amazon or your library might be able to order them for you.

The Report on Unidentified Flying Objects by USAF Captain Edward J. Ruppelt.

The UFO Experience: A Scientific Inquiry by Dr. J. Allen Hynek.

Project Identification: The First Scientific Field Study of UFO Phenomena by Dr. Harley Rutledge.

Clear Intent by Barry Greenwood and Lawrence Fawcett.

The UFO Enigma by Dr. Peter Sturrock.

UFOs and Government: A Historical Inquiry by Dr. Michael Swords and Robert Powell

Unidentified: The National Intelligence Problem of UFOs by Larry Hancock

Unconventional Flying Objects by NASA aeronautical engineer Paul Hill.

Lastly, learn more about the night sky. Become familiar with the stars, planets, comets, and meteor showers. Learn how planes, helicopters, and Chinese Lanterns look at night. This knowledge will help make you better prepared to understand what is explainable and what is not.

GLOSSARY

Note: This glossary is unique to the terms and words used in this book

abbreviation	a shortened form of a word or group of words
agencies	groups within the government like the FBI or CIA
altitude	distance above the ground
analyze	to think carefully about a subject
antennae	a thin long rod-like wire used to pick up a signal
Army Reserve	an Army soldier who also works another civilian job
awe	amazed or filled with wonder
braced	to hold steady
briefed	to tell someone about a certain subject
civilization	a society or culture such as human civilization

coincidence	when something happens at the same by accident and they seem to be related
compass	a device that tells you which way is north
concentrating	to pay a lot of attention to
concerned	to be worried about something
credible	a source or person who knows what they're talking about
darting	to move quickly and suddenly
determine	to find out
develop	to grow
diameter	distance across the center of a circle
dimension	another part of the universe that we can't see
dissolved	to break into smaller pieces
distressed	to be worried or anxious
disturbance	something that is uncontrolled
disturbing	bothering
drones	a remotely controlled machine
eliminates	to get rid of
emitting	to give off an energy or sound
encounter	a meeting or to come upon something

The Truth About UFOs

enlarged	to make bigger or larger
evolve	to develop over time
exoplanets	planets that orbit a star that is not our sun
exposure	to come into contact with something
extended	to stretch out
Extra-Terrestrial	something that has originated from outside of our Earth
filmed	to take a picture of
hoax	to fake or trick someone into believing something that is not true
horizon	the line where the earth meets the sky
Hubble telescope	The first large telescope sent into space to photograph the planets and stars
hypotheses	the plural of hypothesis
hypothesis	a proposed explanation for something that is observed
incident	something that happens or an occurrence
indication	a reason to believe
Infra-red Image	a picture taken in a wavelength of light that is not visible to the eye

inhale	to breathe in deeply
instrument panels	the panel on a jet where the dials, switches, and displays are located
intentionally	on purpose
intercept	to chase and to try and catch
interfered	to get in the way of
investigating	to look for the cause of something
jet squadron	a group of 12 to 24 jets that are controlled by a commanding officer
lieutenant, Lt.	the lowest rank of an officer in the Air Force, Army, or Marines
maneuvers	skillful movements by an aircraft
maximum	the greatest or highest
narrowly	barely or very closely
national security	the protection of a nation
navigation	how the pilot controls the aircraft to get to his destination
numb	can't feel anything
orbits	to travel around a moon, planet, or star
originally	in the beginning
originate	to come from
panicked	scared

The Truth About UFOs

phantom	Ghost-like or hard to see
phenomenon	an event or incident that does not have an explanation
photographic film	a thin film that shows a picture when exposed to light; this is how cameras used to work
prime minister	a British leader that is similar to a U.S. president
pulsating	a light that turns on and off at the same rate
radio	to call or contact someone; also an old method of communication
reflected	when light bounces off something such as a mirror or a metal
reliable	something that you can count on to be true
reproduction	to create a copy of an original
request, requested	ask for
research	to study
retrieved	to bring something back or to get something
revolving	to go around an object over and over
scamper	to quickly leave

scope	an object that contains a lens to make something appear closer when viewed
Senior Chief	a rank below an officer in the Navy; similar to a master sergeant in the Army
solar panels	panels of material that create electricity when exposed to sunlight
Soviet Union	also known as the USSR, it was a group of communist countries controlled by Russia from 1922 to 1991
speed of sound	the speed at which sound moves through the air, usually about 770 miles per hour
spheres	a circular object; a basketball or baseball is a sphere
startling	surprising
unidentifiable	something that is unknown or that cannot be identified
verified	to make certain something is true
whine	a high pitched sound

The Truth About UFOs

wilderness	a natural area of the earth where there are not many people
windshield	the window in the front of a plane or a car
zigzag	to move quickly to the left and then right over and over as you move forwards
zipped away	to leave very quickly

Robert Powell

ABOUT THE AUTHOR

Robert M Powell has a BS in Chemistry and is an executive board member and founder of the Scientific Coalition for Unidentified Aerospace Phenomena Studies. He has studied the UFO phenomenon for the last 13 years and has authored multiple papers on the subject. He is a co-author of the book *UFOs and Government: A Historical Inquiry*. Robert currently resides in Austin, Texas.

CPSIA information can be obtained
at www.ICGtesting.com
Printed in the USA
LVHW081117161220
674005LV00006BA/658